she blooms like roses
stretching toward a summer sky
her skin like the air
her voice like the wind

she flows like words
from a poet's mouth
reciting all the things
that maybe only she
knows about

hidden like a secret garden
you'd be lucky if you find her
growing on her own
in search of everything
that they denied her

strong and deeply rooted
she belongs to herself
swaying beneath the sun
as she blooms for herself

her silence was deafening
her whispers held the strength of hurricanes
the sound of her heart shouting
was atomic enough to level cities

regardless of what tool of expression
she'd use, she was bound to be heard
and she demanded that you listen

hear her..

I think the same strength you've been using to hold on to a relationship that no longer deserves your effort can also be used to free yourself. I believe that if you're strong enough to stay in a relationship that feels like hell then you're also strong enough to be alone. Single until you're ready to try again. Single until you've found the type of love that makes your soul feel free.

Don't let your ex distract you from replacing them with someone better.

I think you're just tired of caring about a person who refuses to treat you the way you deserve. I think you're just so fucking tired of wasting your time thinking about someone who never keeps you in mind. I think you're just trying to build enough courage to walk away for good and I believe you will.

Fuck him, for making promises with your heart that he never intended to keep. Fuck him, for placing this heavy emotional burden upon your soul. It's okay to be upset, it's okay to be angry. I know the world wants you to be polite about your pain but fuck that. Feel whatever you need to feel. Shout your truth if that's what will make you feel better.

she has warrior blood
and the soul of a winner

she gives everything she has
because she knows that on her own
she will make it
and she always does

I hope you find a relationship that gets you closer to the type of relationship you consider to be goals. I hope you find the type of relationship that brings you closer to the love your heart desires.

Sometimes being alone feels more like a gift. Sometimes solitude is a peaceful and inviting space. You owe it to yourself to remove your attention from anything that causes your heart to ache. Find a place where it is easier to focus on what brings you joy and stay there. Even if it means being lonely for a bit.

You're tired of being placed in a space where you find yourself having to fight with him. You're tired of the conflict and the confusion. You're tired of trying for someone who refuses to make the same effort as you. You're tired of the heartache that follows you into the night, making it difficult to fall asleep. You're tired and yet you're restless. You're tired and yet you continue to hold on because you hope things will get better but it won't. No matter how hard you love him, he'll never deserve you and if you're reading this now…if you're relating to everything i just said then you have to know that this guy you've devoted yourself to doesn't even love you because if he did, these words wouldn't have spoken to you in such a painful way.

You can't love a person into loving you and no amount of effort will make the wrong person your soulmate. I think you're having a hard time because you've placed expectations on the one person who you can't depend on. You're holding on longer than you should because of all the time you've invested but it's important to recall all the time you've wasted on loving someone who is only committed to hating and hurting you. I know it's difficult because you care and yes, it'll be hard because your feeling are genuine but you'll never be happy while holding on to the person who is constantly giving you reasons to walk away. There is love in letting go, there is so much peace in moving on from the person who can only offer you chaos. You can't love a person into loving you but you can love yourself enough to move forward without them.

There is someone searching for someone with a heart like yours. Right now, that person is thinking about you even when you're up, overthinking, restless and heartbroken, wasting your nights on the idea of someone who isn't even worth thinking about. There is someone waiting to give you everything the others have denied you and i hope they find you when you're ready to be loved by the right person.

This idea that being unhappy means that something is wrong with you just makes you even more unhappy. You're chasing this high because you think those lows don't matter but everything you feel is significant. Every scar matters and each heartbreak is a lesson. You're not okay and that's fine. You're not okay but you will be. Don't run from the sadness but don't accept this idea that happiness is something you always have to feel because you don't. There will be moments of joy, there will be moments where you feel like everything is going wrong. No matter what it is, just know that you are fully capable of handling all things. In all things, no matter what, never forget your strength.

You may never forget him but you will find a way to survive without him because you are capable of giving your heart whatever it needs and I think right now, your heart deserves a permanent break from his lies, his disloyalty, his bull shit.

the moon waited up all night for her

you're the type of imperfect
that someone needs

to be the only one you see a future with
to be the only one you choose for life
for love

sometimes you find a home in a person and leaving feels impossible

you will always be a poem worth reciting
out loud

she was the girl
that no one could keep
because she refused to stay
where she wasn't loved

she was the girl
who wanted to run
through fields of flowers
with her toes in the dirt
 and her hands to the skies

she wanted to feel freedom
running through her hair

she was the girl who daydreamed
of a love that didn't end up
being a nightmare

forever was just another lie
on the way to heartbreak

and you've been losing yourself
just to win over someone
who isn't even a prize

maybe you are a good person
i just wish
you could have been
good to me

so much of you
exists in my dreams

some homes are human
some humans feel like shelter

no more giving everything
to the one person who makes you feel like
nothing
no more attempting to fill yourself
with someone who will leave you empty

no more forcing love in places
where your heart doesn't belong

loving the wrong person is a potent drug
an emotional addiction
as much as you wish to quit
you often find yourself stuck

but there will come a moment
where you build up the courage
to knock the habit of holding on
to someone who doesn't deserve
to have a hold on you

What type of lies are you telling yourself in order to keep holding on to a person who obviously hates you or treats you like they do. Tell yourself the truth, be honest with yourself. You deserve it. You deserve the realization, this understanding that you are far greater than these toxic relationships.

i'm running out of places
 to hide this pain
i'm running out of happy lies
i'm running low of energy
to keep pretending

it's a terrible thing
remembering the good times
with the people
who mostly treated you badly

like the last page of a book
i found myself finally finished with you

it's a funny thing

i don't hate you
i don't care

choose someone who craves the melody in
your voice and the light from your presence

It's the little things. Someone's concern for whether or not you had a meal that day. Someone who genuinely wants to know how your day was. Someone who would do anything to support your quest towards happiness. It's the little things, those little things that reveal just how much a person cares for you.

I was no longer willing to ruin myself while trying to fix you. This is when I realized that I was ready to let go.

It's okay to forgive others without the intention of giving them a second chance. You can accept a person's apology while leaving the door closed for good.

do not exchange the peace in your soul
for the chaos disguised as love

some relationships are hell
don't let these devils haunt your heart

People leave and all the things they did to you and made you feel, seem to stay. Maybe that's what hurts the most. Feeling forgotten by the person you'll always remember.

You've always wanted the joy of being sure
about someone who is certain about you.

You were relying on the wrong people, weren't you? Placing your trust on weak shoulders. Believing in people who have never showed up. You insist on depending on the words of someone who'd rather lie to your face, denying your soul of the truth you long for. You put everything on the line for them and somehow it meant nothing. So here you are, still standing on your own. You placed hope in a place where it would vanish and now you only rely on yourself.

I get it..

You should have left his ass a long time ago.
All those second chances to do better but
instead he's decided to hurt the one woman
who has always had his back. The one
woman who he doesn't even deserve, you.

I get it. You read my words and sometimes these words make you feel good but that's not the point. I'm not trying to provide some temporary fix. The likes are cool, the comments are fine. I appreciate you buying my books, I appreciate the support but I actually want you to be happy. I'm hoping to spark this idea and or remind you that you are better without the person you thought you needed. You are better without the person who has decided to hurt your heart. Don't just like this shit, live it. Apply it to your life! I just want you to be happy...

you're tired of crying thunderstorms
but your pain matters
don't hide it

Love is making time where there is none.
Love is telling the truth even when a lie is
more convenient.

Your soulmate is waiting for you to walk away from the person who chooses to hurt you.

(this was an idea that got me through so many tough times and while no one will save you but yourself…it's nice to know that there is someone out there who is capable of caring for you properly.)

We were never meant to make it and you
were never the person you claimed to be.
Your love was just a lie and I deserved more
than you were willing to give.

You felt like home in the beginning. You felt like hell towards the end.

I learned that no matter how hard you try.
You can't make a soul mate out of a person
who is incapable of loving you correctly.

I was tired of starting over and so I held on longer than you deserved.

There's the first person you claimed to love and then there's the first person who helps you discover the type of love that has no end. And even though they're not the first, they end up being the last person you fall for and that's the love that actually matters. That's the love that never dies. I hope you find a love that redefines what you thought love was.

I knew you'd do the exact thing you promised you wouldn't. I knew you would later reveal yourself as everything I've struggled to avoid and yet I still allowed you in, knowing that my soul would become weary once I saw your true colors. I'm tired of starting over then starting with the very person who is destined to push me toward the end of my rope and still I hold on to this hope of finding love where it'll never existed. I'm pissed at myself for letting you in. Another lover turned liar, another moment of emotional destruction that I could have avoided but I didn't because I got tired of feeling lonely and even that's not a good reason or excuse because all this time that we were together. Loneliness was all I felt.

I was always happier without you. In time, I realized that I was never truly in love with you, I think I fell for the idea of having someone and I forgot to place importance on having someone who could actually care for me in a way that would make my soul smile. I was happier without you but It was even more obvious in the weeks that came after the break up. You reached out and I ignored it, I didn't give in and respond. You reached out again and I decided to block your number. You reached out through another phone then I decided to change my number. You held on to this hope of me being weak enough to let you back in but then I began to love myself and eventually I moved on. I was always happier without you and now I'm much happier with someone better.

Time is a fickle thing. You can be with someone for years and never know what real love is and fall in love truly and completely after weeks spent with someone who literally redefines what it means to be happy. Love doesn't always fit into a timeframe. Remember this.

You tell stories with your eyes, I look at you
and see a truth that feels like everything I've
been searching for. Pain has had its way
with the both us, I see your scars, I'll show
you mine. Isn't this poetry. The way we
exist in this moment, my fingertips like
magnets calling out to you. The palms of my
hands longing for yours. You tell stories
with your eyes and maybe this is the
beginning of our chapter.

I wish to be unseen, I long to vanish behind the noise of this city. The overcrowding streets, the chaotic melody of cars rushing through traffic. All the people talking. Their earbuds blasting music or the gentle voice of someone who couldn't make it out. All of this is going on and all I long for is to be unseen. I want so badly to vanish behind the shadow of New York City.

I was always loving without being loved. I always found myself caring while feeling neglected. It was tough but I was tougher. It was difficult but I moved forward. There is a form of therapy in facing the terrible truth and even though terrible things often happen to the best people. The people who know the sharp edges of heartache are much stronger after the break down.

Being alone is not a punishment
Being alone is not a punishment
Being alone is not a punishment
Being alone is not a punishment
Being alone is not a punishment
Being alone is not a punishment
Being alone is not a punishment
Being alone is not a punishment
Being alone is not a punishment
Being alone can be freedom
Being alone can be eye opening
Being alone can be a gift

Are you taking care of yourself? Are you being gentle with your own heart? You've been through so many things, you've been fighting for so long and I believe that it's time for you to take a break, to get some rest. I'm not telling you that the fight is over but maybe you need a moment to recharge before resuming the fight and that's completely fine.

So many people are capable of loving the wrong person so profoundly. Just imagine the depth, value and power of that love when finally shared with the one person who is readily willing to give that love back.

you are
your greatest gift
not everyone deserves you

I'm no longer willing to chase people because chasing after a person would imply that they've left and anyone who is willing to leave me was never worth keeping.

You said I changed but I don't think that's the word you're looking for or maybe it's not the word I prefer. Yes, things are different and so am I and though change is good. I EVOLVED and that's better.

The silence that lives in the moment of heart break will be the loudest thing you'll ever here but eventually you survive it. Eventually you get to this place of peace.

you have this undeniable strength
living beneath your skin
inside of your bones
and i wish you'd trust it

i was love drunk
from her whiskey kisses
nothing could sober me
from her touch

because if you know
what it means to be broken down
you also know what it means
to be strong in a world
that expects you to be weak

so much of what forever means
is composed with beautiful lies

she emerged from the fire
unharmed and unbothered
transforming into a flame
they could never put out

you're confused
but if they actually cared
you'd be certain
and if this was truly love
there'd be no need to question it

you are my worthwhile
you are the one thing
worthy of me

uncovered truth
beneath a midnight of trouble
i feel everything at night
i see clearly during darkness

there was freedom
in letting go
and the moment she left him
she discovered her wild

the deepest of depression
lives in the moments
where you're unsure
of what you're feeling
where there are no words
to describe it

love was never her weakness
love was just a strength
that she'd wasted on weak people

all she wanted was to be seen
by the right person
she was tired of hiding
her heart

all this time
she was the sun rising
constantly lifting herself
above this world

she wanted you to prevent your ex
from standing in the way
she wanted you to choose her
over the women who existed
in your past

she wanted to be the only woman
in your life but you complicated
something so simple

you didn't actually want me
you just wanted someone
you were never in love
you just needed something to do
and you never truly missed me
you were just tired of being alone

we choose the company
of those who make us restless
then wonder why
our nights are sleepless

behind her smile
lived a profound sadness

despite the fear
she chose to fight

despite the pain
she decided to survive

Made in the USA
Middletown, DE
29 May 2018